To _____

From _____

Other giftbooks by Helen Exley:
The Love Between Grandmothers and Grandchildren
To a very special Grandson
To a very special Granddaughter
To the World's best Grandma
An Illustrated Grandmother's Notebook

Published simultaneously in 1997 by Exley Publications in Great
Britain, and Exley Giftbooks in the USA.

12 11 10 9 8 7 6 5 4 3 2 1

Copyright © Helen Exley 1997
The moral right of the author has been asserted.
Border illustrations by Juliette Clarke.
Edited and pictures selected by Helen Exley.

ISBN 1-85015-799-5

Exley Publications Ltd, 16 Chalk Hill, Watford, Herts WD1 4BN, UK.
Exley Giftbooks, 232 Madison Avenue, Suite 1206, NY 10016, USA.

A copy of the CIP data is available from the British Library on
request. All rights reserved. No part of this publication may be
reproduced or transmitted in any form or by any means,
electronic or mechanical, including photocopy, recording or any
information storage and retrieval system without permission in
writing from the Publisher.

Pictures researched by Image Select International.
Typeset by Delta, Watford.
Printed and bound in China.

GRANDMOTHERS

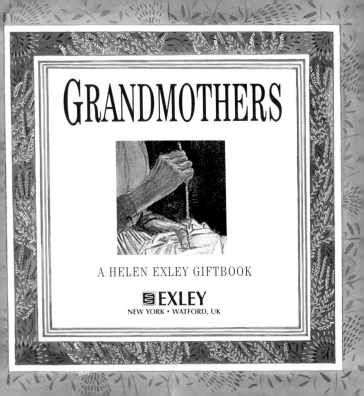

A HELEN EXLEY GIFTBOOK

EXLEY
NEW YORK • WATFORD, UK

It's not just snuggling quietly,
And rocking in her chair –
But Grandma's house is special
Because my grandma's there.

MARIAN BENEDICT MANWELL

I loved their home. Everything smelled older, worn but safe; the food aroma had baked itself into the furniture.

SUSAN STRASBERG

... in the home my grandmother created, I find the beginnings of the love I have inherited.

LOIS WYSE, EXTRACT FROM *"INHERITANCE"*

If nothing is going well, call your
grandmother or grandfather.

ITALIAN PROVERB

On top of material things, every child
needs love, respect, and a bolt-hole when
things get difficult. That's what
grandmothers are for.

CHARLOTTE GRAY, b.1937

When it seems the world can't understand,
Your grandmother's there to
hold your hand.

JOYCE K. ALLEN LOGAN

I wish every frightened, lonely, sick, bewildered child in the world had a grandmother to run to.

PAM BROWN, b.1928

When I fall and cut my knee
she takes me in and laughs. I love her
gentle loving touch, it makes me
feel so safe.

KAREN WILSON, AGE 10

Grandmothers can always be counted on to produce sweets, cookies and candies that seem to taste nicer from her than from anyone else.

ELIZABETH FAYE

Some grans smell of lavender soap, some grans smell of French perfume. My gran smells of pastry and new bread and peppermints. My gran smells gorgeous.

PETER

THE LIGHT OF MY LIFE

... I am very much my grandmother's child. I was willed this sense that your elders are your gods on earth. I would have walked behind my grandmother carrying an umbrella if asked.

LISA JONES

Ever since I can remember my grandmother has been a most wonderful example of fun, laughter and warmth.

H.R.H. THE PRINCE OF WALES

Simply to be in my granny's presence, content and without tension, was sufficient demonstration of love. Her spirituality shone like a lamp from within. When she moved from a room, it was as if the flames of the fire had grown smaller, or the light had been lowered.

MOLLY PARKIN, b.1932, FROM *"MOLL: THE MAKING OF MOLLY PARKIN"*

If I ruled the world I would give her two big fields of roses.

PAUL McAULEY, AGE 7, FROM *"TO THE WORLD'S BEST GRANDMA"*

A granddaughter is a kind of miracle. A persuasion machine. You can try to be strict but you can never resist her smile. You can swear you'll not give her your apple pie, but who wouldn't give in to her toothless grin! You can swear that you'll never buy her another teddy bear, but no one knows your crumple buttons better than she. A tug on your fingers, a little cuddle, a single tear and her *coup de grâce,* a hesitant "Please Grandma, I love you." And with that she can have the world.

HELEN EXLEY, b.1943

In all the old stories grandmothers taught their little children to crochet and knit and sew a fine seam. They existed in cosy kitchens, warm and fragrant with the smell of spice buns and newly-baked bread and freshly-laundered sheets.

A dream. Comforting – but a dream.

For nowadays Grandma is probably in jeans and baggy sweater and can't sew to save her life. Her hair can be any shade in the spectrum – and she irons as little as she can. However, she's handy with a spade – and last week she shifted the furniture around and stripped and papered the living room entirely on her own.

She sometimes knocks together a batch of scones when the grandchildren come to call – but is just

as likely to have got them from the supermarket.
For she's busy, she's got her art class and her course
in car maintenance.
If, of course, she's not running a business or
writing a novel or organizing a protest or
preparing to sail round the world.
But she's just as much a grandma. She'll give the
grandchildren a good grounding in politics and
healthy eating. And how to mend a fuse. And
how to make a genuine pizza.
Her hugs are just as loving – and she's just as
good at stories and secrets – and having a quick
word with Dad.

PAM BROWN, b.1928

GRANDMOTHERS preside over the great family festivals and celebrations – Christmas, Easter, Yom Kippur, Hanukkah. They bind us to the great occasions of life, birth most essentially, but death and, of course, weddings. They are repositories of homely wisdom and accumulated experience. They are bountiful; good things emanate from them. Above all, grandmothers are the civilizers of grandchildren. They enable grandchildren to extend their imaginations beyond the often claustrophobic confines of the so-called nuclear family.

PAGE SMITH,
FROM "OLD AGE IS ANOTHER COUNTRY"

A GRANDMOTHER IS BORN

*Upstretched arms make grandmas put off
rheumatism till tomorrow.*

JULIE B. JONES

*There is a delight, a comfort, an easing of the
burden, a renewal of joy in my own life,
to feel the stream of life of which I am part
going on like this.*

BETTY FRIEDAN, ON BEING A GRANDMOTHER

It is as grandmothers that our mothers come into the fullness of their grace. When a man's mother holds his child in her gladdened arms, he is aware of the roundness of life's cycle; of the mystic harmony of life's ways.

CHRISTOPHER MORLEY (1890-1957)

Grandchildren are a renewal of life, a little bit of us going into the future.

HELENE SCHELLENBERG BARNHART

Most young people today live in a world that is very much like a movie set. Nothing is permanent; everything is a sham. There are very few things we can put our faith in.... Fashions change with every season and whim. In the midst of all of this change and the uncertainties surrounding it, the sights and smells of grandma's house are a stabilizing and important influence. Even the most cynical and jaded young people are brought back to a revaluation of their values and life directions in the midst of these family traditions. Grandparents are the centrepieces of these memories.

JAY KESLER, FROM *"GRANDPARENTING: THE AGONY AND THE ECSTASY"*

LOVE IS BLIND

I suppose you think that, as a grandmother, I might be prejudiced about this particular baby, but my years as a journalist have made it possible for me to observe objectively, and in so doing, I have to admit that Joshua Lee Bloomingdale, at age fifty-three minutes, was the most beautiful baby God ever created.

TERESA BLOOMINGDALE, b.1930

Every grandmother has a drawerful of strange crayon drawings and oddly spelled letters that she wouldn't swap for the Kohinoor diamond.

MARION C. GARRETTY

If only the Ugly Duckling had had a grandmama, he need never have suffered. She, of course, would have seen at once that he was swan material.

PAM BROWN, b.1928

B. Cook

Just how ambitious was Grandma Jones when it came to her grandchildren? Well, when a stranger inquired as to their ages, she replied, "The doctor's in the third grade and the rocket scientist is in the fifth."

ANONYMOUS

I hang out with a lot of grandmas. Their grandchildren were all born in mangers and have I.Q.s so high they cannot be measured.

ERMA BOMBECK, b.1927

Grandmother: "Did I tell you about my grandchildren?"
Friend: "No, and I appreciate it very much."

MILTON BERLE

DOTING GRANDMOTHERS

*Y*ou know a grandmother is a goner on her grandchild when she:
– Nurses every sniffle as if it were life-threatening...
– Frames all outstanding report cards...
– Swears that "Goodnight Moon" is her favorite book.

GRANDMA JAN

No cowgirl was ever faster on the draw than a grandma pulling baby pictures out of her handbag.

ANONYMOUS

If your baby is "beautiful and perfect, never cries or fusses, sleeps on schedule and burps on demand, an angel all the time"... you're the grandma.

TERESA BLOOMINGDALE, b.1930

A LADY TO RECKON WITH!

My Nana is awesome!
She is the only one in my family
who can boss my mom around
and get away with it.

JEFFREY, AGE 9

It is very hard to hoodwink
a grandma.

PAM BROWN, b.1928

A grandma looks formidable but
she's the softest inside.

HELEN EXLEY, b.1943

CRAZY GRANDMAS!

I dig being a mother... and of course, as a
grandmother, I just run amok.

WHOOPI GOLDBERG

Grandmas can make funnier faces and more awful
noises than mothers.
Mothers sometimes say it's because grandmothers
have lost their inhibitions.
And sometimes they just groan "<u>MUM</u>!"

CHARLOTTE GRAY, b.1937

Grandmas have peculiar habits. It's their age.

PADDY, FROM *"AN ILLUSTRATED GRANDMOTHER'S NOTEBOOK"*

They will talk for hours and hours, but they do not mind if anyone is listening or not.

TONI SWINDELLS, AGE 11

Grandmothers are supposed to be old
But mine doesn't think so.

HELENA HOUSTON, AGE 9,
FROM *"TO THE WORLD'S BEST GRANDMA"*

POOR OLD GRANDMA!

Never ask a grandma for anything till
she's had a cup of tea.

PAMELA DUGDALE

Grandmas are good at sitting on the
floor to play, but they are terribly
difficult to get upright again.

PAM BROWN

A grandmother gets tired.
You know when the story starts off as
Goldilocks and ends up as the Three
Little Pigs.

PETER GRAY

My wife recently gave "birth" to her first grandchild. Her daughter, I believe, was allowed to play a minor part in the event, but the son-in-law and I didn't even get "walk-on" parts. The new grandmother is thriving... and I, meanwhile, am beginning to assert my rights and confess to spoiling the child a little.

A GRANDFATHER, QUOTED IN *"YOUR GRANDCHILD AND YOU"*, BY ROSEMARY WELLS

It was extraordinary when [my granddaughter] was little, holding her against me and feeling that babies must somehow give something back, absolute love. I have vivid physical memories of holding her against me, the physical sensation of her body and feeling totally free to love her completely, no complications. With my own children perhaps it was more suffocating, but this felt just a freedom to love.

STELLA, FROM *"GRANDMOTHERS TALKING TO NELL DUNN"*

I didn't expect this child to be such a source of affection. He doesn't "give his grandmother a kiss" or even two kisses. Instead his kisses are a rainforest where the rain never stops falling, little soft kisses on whichever bit of my face is nearest at that moment till I say, "Cato no more," and I am almost hysterical with laughter and pleasure. He too, resting between kisses, laughs, and for me there is the pure delight my grandmother must have felt when her great-grandsons tried to pull her out of the stream and she fell backwards convulsed with girlish giggles.

NELL DUNN, b.1936

When you were very, very small you
clutched my little finger in your fist and
captured me forever. You grew and learned
to walk and took me off on explorations.
The shabby autumn garden revealed itself as
wonderland – a last, last rose, a pigeon's
feather, a fat and prosperous worm, a drift
of golden leaves, a scurrying mouse.
Your hands tugged me from my chair, pulled
me to the door, marched me away.
To the park, to the shops, to the library.

The museum. The railroad. The woods.
The beach. The river.
Showing me a world I had half forgotten.
A world full of wonders.
And when you are grown and stride away
and leave us all behind – our hearts will go
with you. To places we have never seen.
To a time we will never know.

PAM BROWN, b.1928

My granny's house with its outside lavvy, its indoor plumbing complete with new bath and running hot water, its coal fires in every room, summer and winter. My granny's house in the minuscule mining village, Pontycymmer, in the Garw Valley of South Wales. The place my heart has always returned to for my happiest childhood memories, and which I only ever thought of as home.

MOLLY PARKIN, b.1932, FROM *"MOLL: THE MAKING OF MOLLY PARKIN"*

Whatever happened to the sweet, grey-haired old lady baking cakes, bottling cherries and pottering in the garden? Certainly, the traditional granny still exists, but grandchildren today are just as likely to have a grandmother who is a high-powered career woman, a global explorer, a working woman who combines tending a home, a husband and a busy social life.... But, though the image may have changed, the importance of grandmothers in the lives of their grandchildren is undiminished.

ANGELA NEUSTATTER

GENERATIONS

Nana tells tales that she was told… when she was a child. Many stories of exciting adventures that happened a long time ago. They did not have the luxuries that we have, but dancing the Lancers in their large living room when the furniture was pushed aside, singing round the piano, telling stories by the blazing fire whilst they ate hot muffins. Skating on the frozen park lake in the winter, riding on the top of an open deck tram car, all these more than make up for television and holidays abroad. I hope my Nana will stay with me for a long time, and when I have the farm I long for, she will be able to live with me and feed the chickens. We will have a blazing log fire and she will tell us stories of the past.

DAWN WILLIAMS, AGE 10

[My grandmother] was the one member of my immediate family who most understood me, or so I thought at the time. Looking back, I think it was not so much her understanding as it was the sheer force of her encouragement that helped me through those years....

LINDA SUNSHINE,
FROM *"TO
GRANDMOTHER
WITH LOVE"*

Grandchildren are the dots that connect the lines from generation to generation.

LOIS WYSE

Grandmas should write down the stories of their lives, however dull they seem to them. For such tales show history as it is – a procession of interlocking lives. A unity. The family of mankind.

CHARLOTTE GRAY, FROM *"AN ILLUSTRATED GRANDMOTHER'S NOTEBOOK"*

Grannie is not asking for any kind of
special recognition. She simply wants
to be herself, doing what comes
naturally to a grandmother: loving
her grandchildren, passing on the
wisdom of her experience, and being
respected, tolerated and understood
by those around her.

JACK HALLAM,
FROM *"TO GRANDMA WITH LOVE"*

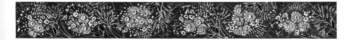

I loved my granny's tiny back kitchen with
its roaring fire and wooden stools.
I felt safe there, sitting against her knees,
watching her perform her domestic chores. I
felt as if I never wanted to leave, that I could
stay there cocooned for the rest of my life.

MOLLY PARKIN, b.1932,
FROM "MOLL: THE MAKING OF MOLLY PARKIN"

SPECIAL LOVE

Grandmothers come in dozens of shapes, bunches of wrinkles, languages, clothes, skins and stages of degeneration. But they all have exactly the same love in the middle.

PAM BROWN, b.1928

Most grandparents, like most parents, love their grandchildren unconditionally, regardless of their achievements.

ELIN McCOY

You will always be there for me and you make me laugh. If I had the world I would give it to you. I will always love you.

MICHELLE WILSON, AGE 9

I think you are very special to me because you helped me grow up. Now you are very old I care for you twice as much.

NICOLA WATSON, AGE 9

So many things we love are you, I can't seem to explain except by little things, but flowers and beautiful handmade things – small stitches. So much of our reading and thinking, so many sweet customs.... It is all you. I hadn't realized it before. This is so vague, but do you see dear Grandma? I want to thank you.

ANNE MORROW LINDBERGH,
FROM *"BRING ME A UNICORN"*

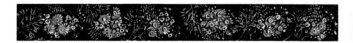

THE ETERNAL HUNTRESS

Grandmothers have always been instinctive scavengers. Always had bags bulging with discovered treasure – swags sewn from deer hide, sacking, cotton and now PVC. And always with something special for the grandchild. Bright berries, a perfect stone, a handful of hazelnuts, an iridescent beetle. A pair of woolly socks. A china-headed doll. A CD. We have moved with the times, we grandmas – from the cave to the modern apartment.

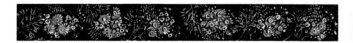

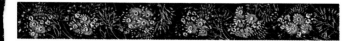

Our eyes sharp as robins – always on the look-out
for something extraordinary, something unique,
something beautiful for our beloved children's
children. For Om and Flavia, Ethelberga, Jane and
Charity, Nell and Geronimo, Sean and Sue-Ellen.
Hoping to see them smile.
Hoping for a kiss.

PAM BROWN, b.1928

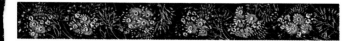

Since the beginning of time grandmothers have been negotiators and peacemakers in their families.

GRANDMA JAN, FROM *"GRANDMOTHERS ARE LIKE SNOWFLAKES... NO TWO ARE ALIKE"*

Grandmas are good at secrets and sorrows and plans and fears.

CHARLOTTE GRAY

Grandmothers are very good at picking up the pieces of something shattered beyond all mending – and mending it.

CLARA ORTEGA, b.1955